Single
PURPOSE

God's Guiding Principle Behind
Waiting Patiently For Marriage

~ Anntwanique D. Edwards, Ph.D. ~

Book Layout & Design:
Tarsha L. Campbell

Cover Artwork:
Garrick Gibson, Creative Consultant

Editing by:
Kandra Albury, Professional Communications Consultant
www.kandraalbury.org

The Life Quotes were taken from livelifehappy.com

Cover image: BigStock by Shutterstock
Interior image: Shutterstock

Published by:
DOMINIONHOUSE Publishing & Design, LLC
P.O. Box 681938 | Orlando, Florida 32868 | 407.703.4800
www.mydominionhouse.com

DEDICATION

This book is dedicated to everyone who yearns to be married and those who struggle to find contentment with being single.

Special honor is given to my grandparents and parents who stood strong during all facets of marriage, underscored by the traditional vow:
"For better, for worse; for richer, for poorer; in sickness and health; till death do us part."

Your gift of more than 140 years of combined marital experience has served as a tool of personal preparation and shall always be cherished.

The Late Mamie and Lonnie Edwards –
50 years of marriage
Clotea and (Charles) Bray – 53 years of marriage
Beverly and Jeffrey Edwards – 43 years of marriage
and counting

"*God has purpose and intention for each of us. His single purpose for us is more than being aware of our status as an individual who is not married. Single purpose is about God being glorified.*"

TABLE OF CONTENTS

"*If our focus moves beyond the outward appearance of man and transcends our limited scope of how love should be revealed, then we may encounter more authentic experiences with love.*"

PROLOGUE

••••••

The Meaning of Love

"Love is a word that comes and goes, but few people really know what it means to love somebody..."

~Kirk Franklin

We all want to be loved. Everyone wants to know that somebody will support them and be there in times of need. We are innately built to appreciate affection from the time we are held in our caretaker's hands at birth and cradled near our mother's beating heart. Babies are quickly exposed to sweet whispers and gentle kisses. They usually are the recipients of endearing warmth. As we get older, we maintain our desire for a sweet embrace and the feeling that everything will be okay because someone loves us. Yet, love is not defined by our emotions and the feeling of safety. Love requires more than we generally receive or extend to others, on a typical day.

Love is a sacrificial action. It requires a sense of selflessness that is generated by giving with no expectation of receiving the same kindness in return. Amazingly, many people have no idea of what love is and get married without ever experiencing its true definition. Thus, emotions can drive some people to make declarations of love. Their proclamation is that they are smack dab in the middle of love. Yet, their love is only about the butterflies in their stomach when they expect a call from their significant other or how their heart skips a beat when he or she enters a room.

Having chances to gaze upon another individual and experiencing breathtaking moments at the sight of them is not the sole indication that lifelong love connections have been made. Overpowering feelings of positive sensations often erupt into vows of affection toward one another in the sight of God while simultaneously struggling to understand the meaning of true love.

Subsequently, people attempt to resolve their relational problems by divorcing themselves from love affairs and making nuptial vows of null effect. Imagine if love could simply be defined by the depth of our cravings or tenderness toward another human. Those connections may be indicative of "falling in love" as humans have described the definition, but it excludes the important elements of God's description. Heaven's definition of love includes total sacrifice. Its description omits the need for divorce as we humble ourselves to be led in relationships by Christ; versus the pitter patter of accelerated heartbeats.

Although we see individuals suffering to uphold love in marriages, many single people are still eager to walk down the aisle as quickly as possible. The intense desire to get married causes people to rush into commitments they are not adequately prepared to manage. Because hearts are fragile and deceitful, some begin finding themselves getting depressed about being single. It is my hope that men and women will begin to appreciate their singleness.

In more than 40 years of being single, or described by some as being *alone*, I have learned that there is magnificence in possessing single status. I know there is Godly purpose in being single and it has prepared me more for marriage than anything else. I have learned the significance of my existence and the purpose for marriage, which is to equip me to be better prepared to handle love. I no longer bear any tears, worries, or disappointments about broken relationships or being single. I am in an extraordinary place, the designed position for future greatness and complete success; the place of preparation. I am ecstatic to be where God needs me at this time in my life.

God has purpose and intention for each of us. His single purpose for us is more than being aware of our status as an individual who is not married. Single purpose is about God being glorified. God's objective is for us to be in relationship with one another, but to also find success in our unions by first being joined with Him. God wants us to have a love relationship with Him, and be in love with a single God called Yahweh. Our first true love must be Christ. To know love and be prepared for marriage is to know the lover of our soul and one who knows our life purpose.

The hand of God shaped us. His breath gave us life. More than any human, God wants to see greatness come out of us. Imagine the flawless plan He sets in action to ensure the future of a radiant marriage that will uplift His kingdom. The ultimate love relationship comes from each partner truly knowing God during their time of being single. Once the foundation is set, God is able to create a unique tapestry of love woven with strength and undeniable power. It is time to appreciate your season of preparation. There is an unmistakable purpose for your current status. Personal contentment is found when we discover that distinct purpose. Those who struggle to locate contentment while single have not tapped into the true purpose for their individual creation.

Love is not a gift to be packaged and repackaged. It is not a tangible item that we can toss around nor should it be one that we look at and decide to like or dislike. We err in the way we view gifts. Similar to love, preconceived notions about its packaging may take the form of incorrect judgments, causing us to misinterpret the actual gift within. Our problem is that we believe we can determine value by looking at the size of gift boxes and bags or by checking the weight. We are all guilty of using these methods of measurement before opening gifts. Inevitably, we are guessing whether we will enjoy the contents based upon how we view the packaging. But, our guesswork may be completely inaccurate.

Consider the plausibility of someone handing you a torn up, wrinkled brown paper bag with undistinguishable black markings on it, only to cautiously open it and find that it contains an extremely valuable, finely-cut diamond ring. Outer appearances cannot conclusively determine the value of what they possess within. We should be careful about our predispositions toward how we think love should be packaged. It is very easy for us to turn love away because we made assumptions about how it should be revealed to us. Just as the diamond possesses value despite the outward appearance of its container, those who may seem unappealing or unworthy of our time may have been chosen by Christ to hand deliver the unparalleled love we have longed for throughout life.

If our focus moves beyond the outward appearance of man and transcends our limited scope of how love should be revealed, then we may encounter more authentic experiences with love. Unfortunately, we tend to measure love through our judgments and previous experiences with others who also have insufficient measuring sticks. Deciding the accuracy of love based on previous negative experiences is problematic. We must align ourselves with the will and voice of Christ; letting Him guide us to places of true love.

God knows which persons possess the most prized elements needed in our life. Certainly, some of us have turned away God's true love because we failed to look beyond the packaging. At times we have denied the best love opportunities because we trusted our knowledge above the wisdom of God. However, God knows us better than we know ourselves. Jeremiah 29:11 states, *For I know the thoughts that I think toward you, saith the LORD, thoughts of peace, and not of evil, to give you an expected end.* God never leads us toward destructive relationships. He always directs us toward His preconceived plan for our happiness. However, our biggest issue is that we follow our defective thoughts and plans instead of God's perfect expectations for us.

The biblical meaning for love is straightforwardly defined as God Himself:

He that loveth not knoweth not God; for God is love
(1 John 4:8)

In as much that God is love, love is God. People who do not know love are not in a genuine relationship with God. Likewise, people who do not fellowship with God are incapable of understanding the essence of love itself. The two are interdependent concepts. To state that we love anyone requires that we must first know God and see Him more clearly than any individual who physically appears before our eyes. Being in love is dwelling within its limitless domain. It is the act of dwelling in the presence of God. *He that dwelleth in love dwelleth in God, and God in him (I John 4:16).* If we are truly in love, we should see God in our partner first and likewise, they should first see God in us.

To explain love as a fundamental experience of emotions, between humans, weakens its true meaning and explains how we so easily change our thoughts about whom we love. Humans like to give excuses about changing their mind regarding love.

15

They say they cannot help who they "fall in love" with because it just happens. Yet to fall is an act of descending, requiring one to move from a high place to a position of humility. It is an example of letting go of self-control and surrendering to a place of God's habitation. Falling in love means we let go of self-centered thoughts and submit to be where God takes us. As crazy as it sounds, that place may not be where we thought we would be or where we think we want to go.

Because love is a surrendering of self, being in love is an indescribable partnership ordained by God. Because God is love, we cannot use love carelessly. Love should not be "a word that comes and goes." When we know what it means, we are more apt to patiently wait upon marriage, a union devoutly sealed by God.

*L*ife Quotes

• • •

"Things take time. The seeds planted do not sprout the next day, but that doesn't mean they never will. Be patient. Things will unfold for you."
– Unknown

" *Sometimes we get caught engaging ourselves in love encounters that are fatal to our spiritual growth and natural progress. These relationships are typically categorized by a preoccupation with another individual instead of fostering spiritual development and focus on Christ."*

CHAPTER 1

• • • • • •

A WAITING HEART

The Bible tells us that our heart is deceitful above all else. Interestingly, people tell us to trust our heart and to follow after it, when in fact they intend for us to follow our intuition. Let's face it, when our heart connects to something, it digs in deep and grabs hold like a bulldog daring anything to try and make it release its hold. The problem with clinching on to what we want is that it may not be what God wants for us.

When it comes to love, we must understand that God intends for us to have and move through the actions of love. Basically, He wants us to have and move through Him, for He is love. As we are guided by God, He helps us hold tightly to those persons whom He places in our path for a love connection. At the same time, God strengthens us to loosen our grip from those who He does not intend for us to be bonded with for life.

It seems like every adult romance movie, as well as fairytales for children, is about finding love. However, media representations of romance depict people who are drawn to one another by emotions. Their personal wants and desires direct their actions. Generally, when they do not get what they want, they either begin to chase after it with more vigor or live in a slump of depression. The idea of love awakens them. Yet, in the wake of love, we must cautiously ask ourselves if we are experiencing a fatal attraction.

Sometimes we get caught engaging ourselves in love encounters that are fatal to our spiritual growth and natural progress. These relationships are typically categorized by a preoccupation with another individual instead of fostering spiritual development and focus on Christ. For some, this concept seems *too spiritual* because we have allowed the world's depiction of love to overshadow God's intention for love. Let us be mindful that placing God in the center of our relationships does not rid us of opportunities to be ourselves or make greater connections with another man or woman. In fact it does just the opposite.

Putting God at the forefront of relationships allows Him to be exalted through every decision. When Christ is at the helm of our heart, He steers while we ride the ship of love, floating upon gentle seas in the right direction. With God as our spiritual captain, we avoid turbulent water and the rocky waves of a disastrous partnership with the wrong shipmate. He helps us understand our companion better. He encourages us to maintain patience even in the most difficult times. When we allow God to be at the center of our union, He guides us toward the happiness that the world craves each day.

It's a pity that our dire cry for love does not always get the response we want. Every person we love is not required to reciprocate our love in the way we hope.

Even more unsettling than searching for unfound love, is sometimes finding it. There are times when we will find what we think we want, even if it is not what we need. Hearts are broken because we do not recognize loving someone does not inevitably mean a lifelong bond. Our hearts may trick us into making dangerous connections with others who have no compatibility with us.

One of the greatest examples of our deceitful hearts is depicted in two old movies, *Fatal Attraction* and *A Thin Line Between Love and Hate*. When considering these movies, people almost instantly think of the crazed women exemplified by the main characters in each film. *Fatal Attraction* underscores the deranged behavior of a mistress who is angered by the betrayal of her lover, a man who first accepted her affection but then abruptly cut off their extramarital escapade. As a repercussion, she goes on a revengeful, crazed rant led by a broken heart. Her emotions turn from joy to rage and her actions follow suit. Her bitterness towards her lover places her in a murderous pursuit of him. The other movie portrays similar examples of emotion-led thinking.

In *A Thin Line Between Love and Hate*, one of the leading female roles finds herself unable to cope with rejection. After her boyfriend disengages from their relationship, she focuses on every negative relationship she has endured in the past. Her bruised heart motivates her to willfully act out of character. Similar to the first movie, we see the heart that once loved is now consumed with hate and produces the most destructive behaviors. Our heart can deceive us into acting in ways that are unbecoming to God. Following our emotions can cause us to reinforce actions displeasing to Christ.

We must learn to trust God and not our emotions. In the movies mentioned above, neither woman took a moment to catch her breath, sit in the calmness of God and seek His direction. Neither willingly accepted her current circumstance and waited for change. From these movies, a prevailing question emerges about the process of waiting: How do we wait when our heart yearns to be filled with love?

The Art of Waiting

To save ourselves some heartache, we must learn to surrender to Christ. He will teach us how to wait on the best relationships for us. God knows we want to be connected in a great partnership. He recognizes our vested interest in becoming married and starting a family because He placed the desire within us. Yet, achieving the goal of marriage is not equivalent to reaching the perfect status in life. We must be careful to fall in Godly love and with the right people. Sometimes, we give ourselves away to the wrong people. Other times, we love the right people at the wrong time, rushing to make unions through our own actions. Trying to find love by chasing after it is not the answer to our longing for love connections. Believe it or not, waiting can be paramount to experiencing true happiness.

Waiting is an art that God empowers us to master. Google provides a definition most befitting of a challenge. Ultimately, it defines waiting as our need to be still. It is described as "the action of staying where one is or delaying action until a particular time or until something else happens." Waiting exemplifies our ability to pause and accept delays that occur in life. To wait is to accept our current, "right now" moments with appreciation, knowing that in due time the future will present what is necessary for that appointed time. When we realize that God has orchestrated time, then we can more readily accept that what we endure in each moment is most appropriate for where we are going. God has an expected end for us that will be revealed (Jeremiah 29:11). That end is great, but it cannot be rushed because of our anxieties.

People wait because they have an expectation that something is about to arrive. One may wait on a bus to pull up to the stop, a package to be delivered, a promotion or graduation to occur, or a baby to be born. In each scenario, the individual anticipates an arrival. In the case of those waiting to be married, they are expecting to be wed to the right individual. In the meantime, they must make themselves ready for the blessing.

We may feel neglected in our period of solitude, but employing the art of waiting allows us to remain patient. Waiting patiently helps us lose feelings of anxiousness. Two important realizations help reduce anxiety: (1) there is nothing we can do to change God's wait time and (2) what we are waiting for will be worth every second that we must endure in our current state. Sometimes, we can become too eager about capturing the greatness of what is approaching us as well as the magnificence in which God intended for it. First Lady Cynthia Robinson said it best for those who have been waiting a long time; we must keep waiting because "God has a special order for us."

First Lady Robinson likened our waiting to those who wait for an exquisite meal made differently than what is on the traditional menu. She says, it may take more time to prepare, but the chef will deliver an entrée that is well worth the time and cost.

The wait time is the period that occurs between where you are now and where you will be when your expectation is manifested. Waiting is the incorporation of every second we have to prepare for greatness. It is the season that God uses to qualify us for our destiny. We must ask ourselves, "Are we qualified for the gift God has prepared for us?" What we have been waiting for is not typical. What God is about to manifest goes beyond ordinary status. We must be ready for what is coming in the same manner that it must be ready to please us. We should each desire a savory, delectable, slow-cooked and chef-perfected blessing!

A true waiter is one who knows what to do with the time that lingers between being seated at a table and actually receiving the meal that has been ordered.

A good waiter knows how to serve with gladness. His or her duties are that of a servant who meets the needs of those assigned to their area. Anyone waiting on God's blessing should focus on serving Christ while they await the arrival of their blessing. Our season of singleness is designed as a special time of service; it should not be viewed shamefully nor be filled with animosity. Waiting is service unto God, adorned with glory. It requires humility. While we are waiting, we should understand a shift will occur. The scheduled time will come when we will no longer be in the position of waiting for marriage. When the time arrives, we will exchange the difficulty of waiting with a new challenge, managing the union.

*L*ife Quotes

•••

*"It's better to be single with high standards than
in a relationship settling for less."*

"The disturbing reality about selecting a potential mate is that we have a tendency to go blind once we see what we want. We are susceptible to losing good judgment when we think we have won a prized companion."

2
CHAPTER

BLIND DATE

S ome people sit on the edge of their seats waiting to get into a relationship; they jump at chances to go out with strangers because they are eager to find a boyfriend or girlfriend who may soon be called husband or wife. Some look for "hookups" with potential marriage candidates. Friends, family and co-workers are asked if they know anyone who is *husband* or *wife-material*. Then, so called "matchmakers" rise to the occasion, trying to help make love connections. These concerned individuals create "blind dates" in attempts to link compatible people who seek companionship.

Sighted persons who are blindfolded have difficulty maneuvering through ordinary tasks. Reliance upon sight puts them at a disadvantage when they do not have use of their eyes. It is scary trying to do something without sight. Blind dates bring anxiety. Typically, because the two individuals do not know what to expect; they are very nervous before ever meeting one another. Each must rely on the ability of a friend or family member to create a perfect union. As frightening as that might sound, it is equally unnerving to think we do a better job ourselves! We seem to think our sight-filled optics yield better results, but using our own range of vision to pick complementary companionship can also be eerie and disastrous. We trick ourselves into believing we know what type of mate is best for us simply through observation. We think our physical attraction to a man or woman is a strong rationale for beginning a relationship. However, we should be cautious of the physical appeal that draws us in because it can adversely impact our sense of spiritual sight.

The disturbing reality about selecting a potential mate is that we have a tendency to go blind once we see what we want. We are susceptible to losing good judgment when we think we have won a prized companion. Our actions become similar to victims of abuse who are inclined to make excuses for the negative treatment they receive. They tend to focus on the good things that were once given to them by their abuser. Their partner may have possessed golden qualities such as taking initiative or being attentive and humorous. Maybe they were hardworking and wealthy or gave their partner sentimental gifts. In any case, a few positive attributes will never be worth the weight of mental and physical mistreatment. Likewise, we turn a blind eye to damaging qualities about our companions because we grow an affinity toward the traits we enjoy during our romance.

Adhering to God's design for our relationships should be more preferable than obtaining the delight of our will. Our personal enjoyment can easily deceive us into becoming partakers of lust rather than love. For a moment, take time to think about the checklist of characteristics we expect our mates to provide for our pleasure. Consider the non-negotiable items deemed necessary for personal happiness. Now pause. Think about people who have entered relationships with someone who had most of the qualities they desired. Box after box may have been checked on their list of requirements, but the relationship may still have turned out to be a catastrophe. Some of the relationships lacked vital components that were never considered. The ingredients for what we need and even desire are held in God's recipe book. Thus, sometimes we overlook or even leave out the integral elements needed to create a happy relationship.

Contrary to our hopes, neither "tall, dark, and handsome" nor "sexy, intelligent, and able to cook" equate to true love. Real love is more than a checklist of attributes. Being attracted to an individual's physical appearance, intellect, or personality does not mean God has ordained the union nor does it mean we can make it successful. Hanging out, having a good time and having endless conversations does not mean marriage is the answer. Ironically, much of that stuff gets in the way of true purpose in a relationship. If we are too focused on the greatness of each other, we can miss the opportunity to uplift God together. Our single purpose is to glorify Christ in every aspect of our life. Becoming preoccupied with things we like about another individual can cause us to lose focus on God and His intention for our life.

When we see what we think we want, it can hinder us from seeing what we need. Unfortunately, many couples lost sight of negative issues revealed early in their relationship because they were so focused on the stuff they wanted. Signs of misfortune are easily overlooked by temporary feelings of delight. Again, getting what we want does not mean we are in love. Remember, love has nothing to do with our selfish desires.

If our heart is confined to the remarkable qualities of our honey, sweetie, or boo, then we may fail to see warning signs for an inadequate relationship.

But, this does not mean we must lower our standards. Our heart must be open to the possibilities of having more than we imagined. God wants to grant us what we desire as we delight in Him *(Delight thyself also in the LORD; and he shall give thee the desires of thine heart – Psalms 37:4).* Ultimately, delighting in God helps our desires align with what He hopes for us anyway. Once we experience God's love, we become more capable of seeing beyond the man or woman who stands in front of us. We begin to take notice of qualities that reach beyond their height, weight, skin color, body type, intellect and other cliché attributes that everyone seems to want. God will begin to help us take notice of how another person gives and shares His love. By grace, God can open our eyes to have more than what's on our checklist for romance. *Now unto him that is able to do exceeding abundantly above all that we ask or think, according to the power that worketh in us (Ephesians 3:20).* If we do not limit God with our short inventory list, He can and will exceed our expectations for marriage.

Observing how a future spouse loves and interacts with others is an incredibly important quality because love requires sacrifice. Love requires thinking of what is best for that special someone before considering self. To be in love with a person represents a willingness to consider the other person first, giving up what we may want for their betterment. To be in love, means showing your sense of selflessness. To love in such a manner is to love as Christ loves us. Plenty of people want to be married but have no idea how to love. Our single status allows preparation for learning how to love within a marriage. If we are capable of mastering our first and best love affair (with Christ) then we will be ready to display love within marriage. The holy union with our future spouse will be an easier road to travel as a result of our encounter with Christ while we are single, and the training He gives us. Without a doubt, our first and best love union is designed to be between each of us and Christ.

God has given us a Savior to whom we should be joined before we consider being united in matrimony with another person. Although our marital status may be declared as single, God expects us to be married to Christ. In our committed relationship with Him, we learn how to accept love. He teaches us to appreciate sacrifice. He shows us how to give and forgive. The Lord directs us in patience and the necessity of listening. He gives instruction and teaches us to follow His direction. With God we learn how to maintain a spirit of humility and submissiveness.

As many eagerly await a wedding, awaiting preparation for the perfect union should be of greater priority. By time we exit our training stage the qualities we desire may change. We may find other virtues more satisfying and necessary. In fact, things we never deemed essential may be placed at the top of our God-inspired list while other attributes become insignificant.

Jesus Christ is the ultimate date. Although we cannot see Him, His love for us is eternally awesome. We should each accept the invitation to keep company with Christ. There is no better blind date than the one we go on with the Lord. No desires go unmet when we build a relationship with Jesus.

" *Likewise, women cannot bless a waiting husband as God intends unless that woman is in a position to invoke happiness. Similarly, men cannot receive the blessing unless they are positioned to recognize the manner in which God prepared the gift for them.*"

CHAPTER 3

· · · · · ·

A GOOD THING

"Whoso findeth a wife findeth a good thing, and obtaineth favour of the LORD."

~Proverbs 18:22

Thing is a term that describes an object without using a specific name. Proverbs 18:22 states that *a man who finds a wife, finds a good thing.* The scripture indicates men may find gems that they do not know how to name. Each of these precious jewels is a virtuous woman, who stands out with qualities that are rare in comparison to others. To the man that is blessed enough to find her, she will be unlike the common woman. To him, she may be difficult to describe because of her overwhelming uniqueness. Her birth name might be Sarah, Melissa,

Shakira, Michelle, Belinda, Jane or Tasha. However, he might not recognize her by her natural name. But, a man will know he has found his beloved wife when he finds God's good within her. The good he finds within her will have the ability to bless him unlike anyone else and will be profoundly called "a good thing".

Women cannot bless a waiting husband as God intends unless that woman is in a position to invoke happiness. Similarly, men cannot receive the blessing unless they are positioned to recognize the manner in which God prepared the gift for them. Therefore, it is crucial that we first know who we are in Christ. Women must know how to be seen as unique treasures. Otherwise, we will be overlooked as potential wives. Finding favor with a God-fearing man requires us to find favor with the Lord first and to take the idea of marriage off our agenda. Seeking God must be our priority then marriage becomes a viable option for future contentment. Our first step should be devoting ourselves to the refining process.

Know Thyself

The state of being single provides time for us to understand ourselves. We must know our habits and understand our mannerisms. Being alone grants us time to objectively view ourselves. In this single season, we do not have another individual to shift blame upon or point fingers at when things go wrong in our household. During the time we spend living as singles, God grants us the opportunity to have a clear picture of our true selves. It is imperative that we use this time to honestly reflect upon the individual glaring back at each of us in the mirror.

Consider the truths that we are able to expose when we are alone. For example, when bills go unpaid, we have to realize that we might not be good at managing money. We could possibly be a person who jeopardizes our financial budget to get things we desire. The path to successful relationships rests in authentic observations of ourselves during single life. For instance, the aforementioned behavior is dangerous and destructive in a relationship. While alone, there is only one person at risk; however, in a marriage mishandling of money could lead to massive problems. Imagine how a future marriage could be exempt from those concerns before vows are taken. We have the chance to deal with our issues ahead of time.

An individual may manage money well but mismanages time, or prioritizes tasks poorly. As a result, he or she may be habitually tardy to various functions. Learning to handle our inconsistencies in advance allows for fewer problems in a union. There is a whole gamut of situations that could be listed for any one of us. Our idiosyncrasies, peculiarities or individual issues could prevent us from being in sync with our spouse. Those willing to sit in the presence of God and avail themselves to His direction will be better prepared for the complexity of marriage.

We should not shun the time God gives us to get to know ourselves. In our single season we have the chance to become more certain of our emotional state. We should be aware of any tendencies to portray joy versus sadness or patience versus impatience. Being alone gives each of us time to develop as an individual. We become more familiar with our likes and dislikes without the complications that could be imposed by considering the opinion of another person.

God is quite capable of revealing our nature to us before we are married. If we truly yearn to be part of a successful marriage, we should take seriously the time afforded us while we are single. We should become keenly aware of our faults and assets during this time. The success of future relationships hinges upon our self-evaluation and humble request of God to help us with those things. We become more productive with the help of God and better suited for prosperous relationships.

While single we have time to focus on prayer. We can develop a close relationship with Christ and begin to understand the purpose God has for our life. The time spent with God during the years of singlehood prepares us for intimacy. We learn how to give and receive affection, stand in confidence, recognize support, become attentive to God's words and direction. Intimacy is much more than holding hands or having a sexual encounter. Intimate relations are about becoming one. Intimacy is expressed when two people co-exist in a manner that evidences great appreciation for each other without conditions. It requires an act of pure love. No one can completely love another person without first experiencing this kind of love with God.

The state of singlehood is very important. Again, what we do during this time helps us to understand ourselves. The state of being single provides an opportunity in life to help us focus on our personal choices, whether good or bad. We have the privilege of making decisions without considering the viewpoint of another person. Being single is time allotted to us to help us find contentment within ourselves. God affords us this time to respond to our own image and establish our own completeness. It is only when this process is complete that we can then pledge any portion of ourselves to someone else.

Knowing ourselves is extremely valuable. The process of acknowledging our shortcomings and being genuine with God is difficult. Most of us want to see ourselves as prized possessions. The truth is we are exquisite masterpieces created by God– Yet, we have imperfections. We can be a little rough around the edges, like an uncut diamond taken straight from the earth, but once refined by Christ we are made more perfect and better prepared to integrate our lives with someone else.

Training in our single season can help us avoid many broken relationships. Some of those relationships fail as a result of using another person to help us achieve wholeness, contentment, or fulfillment. Rather, we should learn to ascertain these attributes for ourselves. We should never use someone else to generate our identity in Christ. Not knowing who we are can invoke confusion within a relationship. Therefore, we must be complete versus torn when we enter into a relationship. Then, we are prepared to serve as a rich asset to our companion rather than a burden. It is unreasonable to ask others to come in our life to accentuate it when we are incapable or ill-equipped to give the same in return. We cannot expect those we are in a relationship with to be responsible for making us happy. We must know how to be happy while we are single. Others should be able to see the joy we have while we are alone and know we have contentment. Then, when our mate arrives, it only gets better!

Instead of hoping for a better life with a spouse, we should realize that life gets better with Christ. When our Boaz (Ruth 2:1-4:13) arrives or when a man finds his good thing, both partners should be astonished by how God has magnified their level of joy, peace, and contentment. Every single person should desire to be confounded by the possibility of

God making life better than it was while they were single. Marriage should take life and ministry to the next level. It is the exemplification of Christ's love for the church and union with His father.

Knowing ourselves releases us to flourish in relationships. It grants us freedom from experiencing a union filled with tears, disappointment, and frustration. None of us are perfect and marriages are not void of defects either, but when two contented single people connect, God gives them more than enough. He is able to bless beyond what either person may have imagined (Ephesians 3:20). Unfortunately, many people appear to lack appreciation for their single status when we should give God glory for helping us to live fulfilled lives now. When we glory in our connection with Christ, we will excel in future relationships with others.

Pursuing a Good Thing

A man who seeks companionship and actively pursues a woman in hopes of finding a wife is likely to find a female to fill that vacant position in his life. However, finding a woman is not the same as finding a wife. Any man can find a woman to call his spouse, but if he desires to do more than give away a title, a more intense spiritual search is required. Women who merely showcase their "Mrs." title differ from women who actually possess the characteristics of a good wife. God expects for man to hunt for his spiritual counterpart, one who exemplifies the distinctive elements constructed by Christ, not his lustful pleasure or infatuation with counterfeits.

God wants men to search for their wives because the act of pursuing denotes the desire to find something of great value. To find such a precious commodity (a good wife) suggests the man has sought her through prayer. Prayer prevents one from wasting time by connecting with incompatible partners. Prayer serves as a safeguard against poor relationships and guides us towards paths for marital bliss. Men must be weary of linking up with women as a result of natural cravings because all females are not prepared to be wives.

A longing for sensuality can distort the perspective of a man, causing him to be ambushed by his own lust. Men must be careful to not fasten their hopes upon their own personal desires. Men should remember that beautiful, intelligent, passionate and even caring women may be good sidekicks, but if they are not prepared for marriage they could actually shatter a holy union. Prayer serves as consultation with God to equip us to see beyond outward appearances. A true man of God recognizes the beauty of Christ within a woman and sees her as a precious life-long partner ready to grow beside him in the word of God.

Men have been entrusted by the Creator to look for a woman with whom he can share his life and ministry. Spiritual men have been blessed with a gift to discern what is good if they remain aligned with the will of God. As a result of prayer, men can find what God wants for them– A good wife. It is the favor of God that grants men who are seeking a good woman, the chance to receive their sought-after blessing. That blessing is a wife who joins her husband in a life of praise, honor and glory unto the Lord.

God orients women toward the service of being a wife through experience and spiritual guidance. But, men who are not careful can get attached to a decent woman who is not a good wife. A woman who appears first-rate can have the capacity to do jobs well, show herself beautiful and witty, yet she may fail to serve her husband as she serves Christ, with sincere unconditional love and honor. A woman unprepared for marriage is not ready to be the helpmate God has ordained for her future husband. Subsequently, the relationship is mediocre at best and will never bring forth the greatest potential from either partner. As a couple, they are not equipped to maximize each other.

Prayerful men, who find their wife while seeking
God, are rewarded with a good thing– A prepared,
God-fearing mate harnessed for the position of
spiritual wife. II Corinthians 6:14 warns us about
being unequally yoked. The scripture refers to
unbalanced relationships among believers and
non-believers, righteous and unrighteous people,
as well as the troublesome communion between
darkness and light. Therefore, a "good thing"
should be found by a good man. Ultimately, a
good partnership is the joining together of a good
husband and wife. Women should not accept the
advances of men who are not prepared to serve as
husbands. Marriage takes lifelong commitment
from two individuals who have invested time
in fellowship with Christ. As women seek God
and await their time to be found, they are being
groomed for life beyond that moment in which they
are discovered by their knight in shining armor.

We search for those things which are hidden from
us. However, there are times when the object is in

plain sight, but overlooked because it is presumed to be located in a place not visible to the naked eye. Typically, those things hidden right before us are unnoticed because we are rushing, emotionally stressed, and or unfocused. Unclear thinking will lead to missed blessings.

There are women who feel they should have been pursued by great men, but were disregarded. God uses those experiences to help women acquire the virtue of patience during their waiting period. A strong bond with the Lord should be created so that it can be imitated in her future marriage. It is not the intention of God that women should help men complete their search. The right man will not neglect the quality of a good woman when God has prepared him to see it.

In Hiding

Women do not have to flaunt themselves before men. The true way to be found is to get lost in Christ.

Men value women in hiding more than those who say, "Here I am, come get me." Single men who have availed themselves to the viewpoint of Christ see beauty distinctly different than those men who only want a trophy wife.

Women should never connect with men who cannot see the essence of their spiritual beauty. If the beauty of a woman is not seen by the one who she desires, then he is likely the wrong person for her. Women should never come out of hiding in attempts to make a man recognize her worth just as men should not quickly secure a relationship with an unhidden woman.

A man who finds a good woman has found the woman who learned to wait on Christ. She patiently awaits her husband in the same manner that the Lord waits upon each of us to receive him as a bridegroom. Through her close connection to Christ, she has acquired the spirit of submissiveness (not subservience) and learned to walk in humility.

She has learned the importance of accepting unconditional, sacrificial love and knows how to give such love back in return. A woman who loves Christ is prepared to give and receive unconditional love. She is also better prepared to face tough challenges within the partnership of matrimony. A man who can give unconditional love to a good woman will find that she will, in return, give honorable tribute to him and will value all opportunities to lovingly work alongside him.

Strong, goal-oriented, determined women sometimes have difficulty with the concept of giving up their independence. These women tend to have strong leadership qualities and do not like to be taken advantage of or be taken for granted. Yet, this take charge kind of woman must know when to sit back and relax. Like Christ, she must know how and when to use authority with love, gentleness, and kindness. Christ does not have to exert His authority. Through His gentleness, His authority is revealed. Through His humility, He draws others closer. In our relationship with Christ, He teaches strong women to not be overbearing. He teaches them how to best utilize their power. Single women must yield to the secret place of safety; the Pavilion of our Almighty God. Imagine the treasure a good man will find when he looks there! Therefore, women must remain hidden to be found.

Positioned in the Pavilion

The best hiding place for anyone is in the Pavilion of the Almighty. To hide under the Pavilion of God is to rest in a place of safety. One might ask what are you hiding from and the indisputable answer is- from the pain of a broken heart. No one wants to be crushed by the loss of love, irreconcilable relationships, unmet dreams of God-infused unions or the like. We want to be protected from experiences which have the potential to break our spirit.

We can join with more than one individual and find a successful relationship in the same manner that we can have multiple failures with varying persons. We must learn to hide from those partnerships that chase us down as the enemy hunted David. Let's not be foolish, know that there is "spiritual wickedness in high places" that hunts us down to destroy our zeal and fervor to serve God (Ephesians 6:12). The enemy knows that connecting two prepared people in marriage is a threat to him. His best weapon is to attack your heart which you use to love all people, including Christ.

We have to understand the plans and deceptive devices the enemy uses against us. The heaps of broken relationships we experience require constant mourning. The graveyards we build for our losses get in the way of us building strong spiritual structures for the advancement of the kingdom of God. It is a shame that we do not notice how missing fathers, divorces, deaths, and other losses of love impact our relationship with God.

They sabotage our level of growth and impact the level of our risk-taking. They impede our ability to trust and move forward. They hinder our advancement in new relationships because we run away. We evade hardships. We try to escape pain. We attempt to hide in all the wrong places. But, we must learn to hide in the Pavilion of God whereby His care strengthens us, reveals our character, and encourages us to love fully.

God has vowed to protect us. He is committed to getting us to a place of abundance if we rely on Him. It is time we hide in Christ; this is a place of protection from the enemy in which your future spouse can find you. In this sacred place, our mates can find the person God has enabled us to become through His glory.

"*Despite the wide range of acceptance toward divorce when problems arise in marriage, our sacred agreement with Christ and our spouse is for a lifetime. The weight of a broken vow lies upon the individual who chooses to no longer affirm their promise.*"

CHAPTER 4

• • • • • •

THE VOW

*If a man vow a vow unto the LORD,
or swear an oath to bind his soul with a bond; he
shall not break his word, he shall do according to all
that proceedeth out of his mouth.*

~Numbers 30:2

A vow is considered a voluntary promise. In a wedding ceremony, vows are legally binding oaths made between a man and woman. Moreover, the marital vows are sacred, spoken words offered in the presence of God to symbolize a lifelong commitment. Once spoken with the power of life granted us through Christ, it is sealed in heaven as our duty to obtain. Despite the wide range of acceptance toward divorce when problems arise in marriage, our sacred agreement with Christ and our spouse is for a lifetime. The weight of a broken vow lies upon the individual who chooses to no longer affirm their promise.

Let us take a moment to look at typical vows made between a man and woman during a wedding ceremony. In an assembly gathered for the hearing of nuptials, men and women pledge that they will be faithful, loving, comforting, and willing to remain true to one another. Many go on to affirm they will give honor and respect and further promise to remain committed through better or worse, in sickness or health, and whether rich or poor until parted by death. Then the vows are sealed by the authority of a minister and the couple is declared husband and wife. Yet, current divorce rates tell us the error of human ways and show how many well-intentioned vows become vain babblings.

The season in life that we are single provides us with benefits. For instance, it is a great period of time to learn how to balance celebratory occasions with difficult circumstances. Our sole dependence on God in this season stretches our faith and those encounters brace us for what we may endure with another individual. Faithless persons who have not learned how to depend on God by themselves may struggle when trying to seek Him with and for their spouse. As a result, keeping the sacred marriage vow may be a cumbersome task.

Work Through It

God uses our time of being single as a practice ground for exercising faith in Him. He wants our faith to be at a level where we can fully and completely trust Him for all things concerning our life. Our trust in God cannot be based upon the relationship a spouse has with Christ, any more than it can be based on the relationship a grandparent has with Him. We must know the Lord for ourselves. Of course there are people who marry early and grow together in Christ. Some have great success at young ages, but unfortunately they are in the minority. It is hard to grow and understand the changes of someone else when you don't yet know yourself. We should value the time God grants us to know ourselves better.

While single, our devotion to Christ should show evidence of our commitment, and as a result, God will be well pleased with us. Just as we exercise in the natural, our spiritual life requires stretching and strengthening. We start in small places of faith and build until we become stronger. We have to get our faith in shape. In marriage, faith is needed for more than one person. We need to trust God for our husbands, wives and possibly children. The successful marriage contract requires an "us" vs. "me" level of faith. The thought process of the couple must switch from personal to team conscious.

Husbands and wives are designed to be ministry teams who practice faith collaboratively. They each bring their own personal ways of seeking God to benefit the needs of those to whom they are called to reach. Together they pray for direction, knowing God is able to respond. Their partnership allows them to advance to new spiritual territory and together they bring forth balance. Although each person may have an area of weakness, they establish strength together.

We should not blame God because we're not married. Single status is not a worthless position. It is a phase in life that we work through as we approach chances to share new experiences with an extraordinary individual capable of supporting us. We are in training.

While single, our faith towards God develops. During our season of training, as a single person, we should see the positive results of possessing greater faith. We have time to notice how our individual faith is a blessing in the areas of finance, health, and communication. Having a greater level of faith can produce a stronger foundation of encouragement for a couple to come together and trust God with their household budget, physical health of a child, job promotion for a spouse, purchasing a new home, debt cancellation, stronger communication, etc. These areas can become problems that destroy relationships when each spouse is not grounded in faith, however, when both parties enter the marriage union with a strong foundation of trust in the word of God, their combined faith becomes twice as strong to trust God for direction and overcome obstacles.

We should never despise small beginnings because it is just the beginning of a good work (Zec. 4:10). Today, we may be by ourselves, but consider this to be the season of you. We each have our own season and can use it to grow in Christ. Our season should be a pedestal of trust. During this time, we should trust God with our whole being so when someone else comes into our life we will not struggle to believe God for more. This time of preparation will relinquish us as an asset in our future marital union. Our first vow is to be devoted to Christ.

Every fraction of what we learn in our individual season will establish the strength needed to maintain the vows we make to a future husband or wife.

Vowing Communication

Vows that are broken become meaningless strings of words that serve as fuel for heated arguments. Partnerships require communication that negates empty promises or recited phrases at a ceremony. The worth of our words becomes deflated when not communicated in sincerity or backed by effort. While single, God teaches us how to communicate in our relationship with Him. Our union with Christ allows us to experience the best interchange, thereby we are not stuck "giving it the old college try" in marriage. Communication is a skill that must be practiced.

We all have valuable experiences with communication whether deemed good or poor. For example, I can admit to having more than my fair share of failed attempts at communicating my thoughts and feelings. Unintentional problems arose from misunderstandings in less than exact tries at verbal discourse. Positions in leadership, the counseling arena, and other areas of my life helped me to see my strengths and weaknesses during conversation, but none have provided greater clarity than the period of silence required by my audiologist.

My goal was to check my hearing during a free screening. To my surprise, the audiologist was also a certified speech pathologist. In our first encounter, he asked what happened to my voice. He said he listened to me speak while I was checking in and knew a problem existed. This led to a series of questions and treatment that I was not looking for with an ear doctor. Low and behold, I was on my way to learning more about my speech, hearing, and overall communication.

The audiologist quickly recognized the damage regarding my voice. Before taking other measures, he required a period of rest from talking. Fasting from speech is an enormous task for an extremely talkative person, but it was required for the benefit of my vocal health. I accepted the seven day challenge of resting my voice, but imagine the simultaneous challenge of resting my ears!

After completing some tests, the doctor was alerted to an unexpected result. He said there was a dip reflected in the chart indicative of an auditory processing problem. He required that I consider the noise level I was exposed to, and try to lessen it if possible. After doing so, I returned to his office the following week to recheck the results. The outcome was the same. Although I had been exposed to loud noise in choirs and church services, the dip was out of the ordinary. I am able to hear within normal range, but the manner in which I process sound may differ from others. As we discussed my speech and hearing, my learning curve for communication exploded. Finally, I understood more of my personal behaviors...And like lava from a dormant volcano, knowledge erupted in my life and a keener awareness about how people relate to one another began to flow.

We must learn to communicate in a more meaningful and supportive manner. Without first knowing ourselves, we cannot express our needs to others. A disadvantage is our inability to state what we need to feel supported. The key for success in many marriages is in learning how to effectively communicate while single. We could all wait until we are married before trying to figure it out, but imagine how many more couples would experience peaceful homes if effective communication was mastered from the beginning.

Again, we can use my personal experience as an example. I understood the benefit of resting my voice, but I knew it would be a difficult task. I told the audiologist I would try but he said trying was not good enough. For my own sake, he required me to vow to silence. With great apprehension, I agreed. I could not fathom how I might communicate in silence at work so I thought using vacation time to stay at home would make things easier. Unfortunately, my thinking was somewhat erroneous. Changing our pattern of behavior is tough no matter where we are located.

Although we make commitments to change our method of communication with those we love, we find common behaviors are difficult to overcome. Change takes more than a willing heart and a few days of practice. True transformation results from ongoing persistent attempts at using new methods of interacting with one another. We must constantly remind ourselves of the benefits of change although the process may involve personal struggle. We cannot overlook options because we are unsure how to begin. Marriage will require new strategies for relating to another individual. Being single actually helps prepare us to manage our transition into marriage. It is the best time to get to know every facet of ourselves; to understand who we are bringing into the union. Imagine how much work it may be for our spouse to learn how to communicate with us if we are incapable of navigating our emotions because we have no recognition of self.

Relationships require more than a conventional list of behaviors and more than one voice being heard. Communication in a relationship demands confidence and unequivocal support so each individual will value the space, style, and words used by each other as intensely valuable. Verbose communicators sometimes give a long string of words that are a waste of time while listeners seem to use more time than necessary to process the conversation. Less wordy persons appear to undervalue conversation; meanwhile, mouthy people can be considered as babblers who lack appreciation for silence. Neither may be correct though. As we experience life as single persons, we must use the blessing of time to understand how we are uniquely designed to communicate with others.

Exploring our personal fellowship time with Christ gives us significant insight about our communication style. We know that love is the priority between Jesus and ourselves, but we may always feel the need to talk to Him in prayer rather than listening. We may recognize when he tries to talk to us we are busy balancing Him with a multitude of other tasks instead of taking a break to listen. It is possible that we only share things with Christ when our emotional state is at its peak or only when we are in need of something. In other instances, people may find themselves always awaiting a word, but never talk to God themselves. Christ is our greatest lover and our treatment of Him is indicative of how we will behave in a love affair with others.

In a relationship, the burden and responsibility of communication cannot be on one person. When one individual carries the weight of communication, they can easily grow agitated. From my personal experience with a week of silence, I was awakened to the frustrations of people trying to change their communication style. Some people wanted me to write everything down. Others thought my efforts in trying to act out words and pointing to communicate was more entertaining than helpful. As time passed by, I grew tiresome of writing; I became frustrated with how long it took to share my thoughts; meanwhile conversations of others went on to the next topic as I was delayed by writing. Family members became irritated when they could not understand what I was trying to communicate. As a result, irritability levels rose as changes in communication differed because we were not accustomed to new methods of relating to one another. Understandably, everyone who gets married is not prepared to make immediate shifts in their pattern of communication either. Therefore, lack of preparation will generally lead to communication struggles. Learning what is required to communicate well and preparing ahead of time are essential for the longevity of a relationship.

My prescribed 168 hours of silence was amusing to my sister at times. When I tried to relay a message to the family, she would intentionally fill in her own sentiments. During that time, she reminded me of a movie, *Dumb and Dumber 2* where Jim Carrey plays the role of a mute patient named Lloyd Christmas. A loyal friend visited him for twenty years until Lloyd suddenly yelled, "Gotcha!" He was pretending to be mute the entire time! It may seem ridiculous, but many people participate in absurd methods of communication for long spans of time. Their actions are an actual handicap to productivity. Many of us accept our customary style of communication and refuse to work toward beneficial changes. Most of the time, we do it because it is easier than change. We should ask ourselves what changes we have been willing to welcome, even from ourselves. We should be asking God to help us make worthwhile changes that will one day secure joyful marriages.

As much as we may hope for a wedding, we should be more envious of being an extraordinarily happy single person. If joy really is contagious, think about the level of happiness that will spread in your marriage if you enter into it with true glee. Although I am single, I am already happy.

During my required silence I realized that I talk and sing a lot when I am by myself. In times of solitude when I was supposed to be completely quiet, I would make a random remark or start singing a song and then say, "oops!", giggle and go back to silence. Being silent all the time takes a lot of stamina. It is hard work. Purposeful silence requires us to constrain our thoughts, extinguishing unnecessary comments about small stuff. Other people can share thoughts that you oppose, but silence provides no chance to respond or retaliate. Silence dictates personal control over our actions regardless of whether there is another precipitating force tempting you to speak.

I have learned to value silence as moments that do not require action. Silence does not illicit personal responsibility to respond. Quiet moments are the instances where life can simply be whatever it is without any interference. In those times, we have the opportunity to reflect and chances to learn more about ourselves. Silence reveals what we know about ourselves and what those around us recognize about us.

During my time of sanctioned silence, I received more personal insight about my character. I gained more knowledge about the environments I prefer and the people I interact with. As a result, the changes I made had a domino effect. People around me tended to make changes too. At times, they were unsure of what to do and thought it was weird, but together we made the best of it. In our expectation of marriage, we have to know change must be part of the plan. We must know who we are now, what shifts we can tolerate, and that we are willing to make necessary changes before we engage in lifelong commitments that will challenge us.

There are times when the enemy tries to engage you in a war, but God reminds us that no action is necessary because vengeance belongs to Him, the battle is His to fight, and He alone will lift a standard (Romans 12:19; II Chronicles 20:15; and Isaiah 59:19). These are basic principles taught early in salvation. The principle behind each scripture is to trust that God will take care of us whether single or married. The Lord wants us to know that He is the one we should lean on in the time of trouble. The same principle prepares us for healthy relationships, urging us not to engage in battles. The better method is to contain our words and seek God for guidance. Practice overcoming terror with the help of God, while we are single, is perfect training for how to possess victory after getting married. Nothing we experience while we are single is purposeless.

If we are unsure of our relational issues, we cannot hold others accountable for the things that drive us insane. If we do not realize how we communicate with others then we cannot expect partners to understand our needs. We must be equipped to share who we really are with our future mate. Simple details relating to communication styles can effect relationships. One person may enjoy having discussion in loud restaurants while their companion may feel more comfortable in a quiet room. One person may prefer speaking on the phone or texting, but the other may believe face-to-face conversations are best. We should know our optimal communication style and personal preferences. We cannot hold others accountable for what drives us berserk when we do not know the reason ourselves. Being single situates us for personal examination. Our alone time empowers us to possibly become transparent with the person we shall marry.

God is making us ready to vow to a partner who will bring glory to the name of Christ with us. Greater than the vow of one man or woman to God is that between two joined souls bringing double glory to His kingdom. The marriage vow is not as much between man and woman as it is between the Creator and creation.

"If marriage is expected to be an endless union then there is no need to hastily engage in a ceremony. Persons who date, become engaged, and expect to be married, should desire an authentic forever."

CHAPTER 5

• • • • • •

FOREVER

"Wherefore they are no more twain, but one flesh.
What therefore God hath joined together,
let not man put asunder."

~Matthew 19:6

Countless women dream of their wedding day. So much so that they even create timelines for marriage. They give themselves deadlines to wed their prince charming and start a family. There are certainly women out there that actually purchase a dress or reserve a high demand wedding location before ever receiving a proposal and in some cases before meeting their beau. Others may think they are insane, but the planning is because of the expectation we all have to share life with someone who loves us.

People use marriage as an indicator of love. To be single for a long period of time is dreaded by many because it reeks of feelings of isolation and disconnection from the experience of true love. No one wants to feel unworthy of love, but waiting longer than others to be wed does not suggest we are less valuable in the sight of God. In fact, it may mean each partner is becoming a greater helpmate. We should think of the time as a blessing God is giving to benefit our future.

As men and women wait for the season of marriage, they may battle personal expectations, biological time clocks and questions posed by those who want to know why they are not yet married. If focus is lost, then it may become mentally draining to try and explain why they are still single. Self-esteem is in jeopardy and confidence is lost when time seems to be fading away and the dream of marriage becomes an unlikely reality. As a result, some folks may feel compelled to rush down the aisle.

We all know of couples that appeared to have just met and before we knew it were engaged and then married. Like a track athlete who sprints in the 100 meter dash, couples are speeding toward the church doors for holy matrimony. Interestingly, marriage is more like a long distance event that should be approached by those who have trained for endurance. Marathon runners include strength regiments and interval training in their preparation program. They note the importance of refueling to have staying power. They are not addicted to the adrenaline rush that comes with dashing down a straightaway. In training, they learn to pace themselves over time. Likewise, unmarried people are preparing for the long race called marriage. Every situation before marriage is purposed to serve as training for those who want to endure.

If marriage is expected to be an endless union, then there is no need to hastily engage in a ceremony. Persons who date, become engaged, and expect to be married, should desire an authentic forever. Typical reasons for people having a sense of urgency to become wed are impatience, desire for sinless sex, meeting the expectations of others, completing their self-generated checklist, anxiousness about growing older, and high levels of enthusiasm about planning one's own wedding ceremony. But in reality, there is no need to rush into forever, because forever is eternal. It will be there, continually sustained with no ending. Forever is available to all those who approach it, no matter the start time.

Marriage is a lifelong commitment. Saying, "I do" confirms the notion that you are ready to be with someone for the rest of your life. Forever is a very long time! Unless questioning the stability of the decision to make a marital vow, engaged people should have the expectation that they will spend the rest of their lives together. This means they should have enough time to get some things in order before making their wedding vows. If the legitimacy of the engagement is weakened by time, then the decision to get married should be questioned.

Although people have the tendency to point fingers at others, the reality is, those things that usually hinder a marriage are caused by the persons within the marriage. Blame is easily attributed to things, situations and other people, but consequently it is how husbands and wives react to negative factors in a marriage that makes the greatest impact. Matthew 19:6, which reads, *Wherefore they are no more twain, but one flesh. What therefore God hath joined together, let not man put asunder,* is often cited as a reference to keep others from interfering in the affairs of a marriage. What if the spouse is the one who's causing the division? Should we solicit advice from others who could negatively impact our marriage? Entering new territory such as marriage can be incredibly difficult to navigate despite how much a couple adores one another.

Innumerable couples devote time in their marriage fixing problems that arise because they were not actually ready to be married. Running to a place for which we are unprepared only leads to hardship when we arrive at our destination. As a result, our growth is stunted and we drudge through certain experiences that should never trouble us. We must be careful about our assumptions because merely waiting for marriage is not indicative of proper preparation for companionship. Just because we wait a long time for something does not mean we are ready for it when it comes.

What we do during our season of waiting is what differentiates our levels of preparation. Those eager to run into marriage differ from those who find contentment in any stage of life. God wants us to graciously accept every position and process we encounter so we may say, *[we] know both how to be abased, and [we] know how to abound: everywhere and in all things [we are] instructed both to be full and to be hungry, both to abound and to suffer need (Philippians 4:12).*

Growing older does not make one better equipped for marriage. Age is not automatically equated with wisdom. Many aged persons do foolish things.

Being open to God's instruction and learning how to love Him thoroughly makes a big difference in making us ready to love someone else. Oftentimes, we attempt to love others first and then try to love God with our misguided principles for sharing love. Although we seek love more than anything else in life, the world struggles with defining love and identifying it even when received. Our misconceptions cause us to mishandle love.

Generation after generation has supported the notion that we should love others as they love us. If someone fails to love us in the manner we believe is appropriate then we feel justified in lessening our feelings toward them. In fact, we try to force our emotions to become negative. We place ourselves in an unloving state because we do not want to be vulnerable or feel rejected. Forcing ourselves to cripple the act of love is unnatural.

True love is not based upon whether we are uplifted nor is it predicated upon wrongdoing. God has created us in His image and hopes for us to love others as He loves us, completely and unconditionally. Luke 6:28 encourages us *"to bless them that curse [us], and pray for them which despitefully use [us]"* because it is an act of love.

Our sinful nature prohibits us from accepting the idea that we should endure the pain someone has inflicted upon us and still offer our greatest treasure (our heart) to them in return. Conversely, the same sinful nature behaves in contradiction with the word of God yet hopes for His constant love and forgiveness. We want God to look beyond our mistakes and love us forever. Even if we fail to do it ourselves, we hold God to the standard of I Peter 4:8 - *And above all things have fervent [love] among [ourselves]: for [love] shall cover the multitude of sins.*

We want God to remain married to us even when we have separated from Him. He mercifully and gracefully accepts us in any condition. With the hope that we will turn toward Him, God reminds us that He is married to us, even the backslider (Jeremiah 3:14). His love is not based upon human emotion. When we "betray" God by not returning the love He has given us, we still want His hand to be extended toward us. Because His love is non-emotional, it withstands every predicament.

With an awesome level of love God welcomes back prodigal sons and daughters who have not necessarily shown appreciation for the blessings He has prepared for us. Our connection with God is the first example of true marriage. It is the practice of both knowing who we are and letting go of our identity at the same time. During a season of singleness we find our identity is more than we could have ever imagined. It supersedes the bodily form we see ourselves as when we look in the mirror. Instead, we get more than we bargained for when we finally check through our spiritual spectacles and see our mortal image has been replaced by the image of God.

Being joined with Christ strengthens us and inevitably makes us better. He is the pure husbandman, showing us that ordained love connections empower us to live life with new fervor. The ideal mate pushes us to grow and helps us move beyond complacency. Indeed, we are better with God than without Him, but not simply because of what He gives us. We are better because of our acceptance of His love and willingness to return true love. In our state of singlehood, God prepares us to understand the sacrifice needed in a true love relationship.

We are imperfect people who should never hurry to bridge our life with another individual who has not first been married to Christ. Marriage is beautiful when God is the center of the marriage. Getting married does not automatically make either person greater. While single and waiting, we should realize that a change in marital status will not in and of itself make us better people. A wedding day is not the absolute beginning of joy in our life.

Marriage is a partnership that requires an abundance of work. It demands sacrifice, patience, support, and love. It is more effective when entered into by unselfish persons ready to commit for the long haul.

Marriage is strengthened when the individuals who enter into the union are whole persons, not divided mentally, emotionally or restrained by those outside of the marriage. Most of all, marriage has greater chances of success when those who are preparing for marriage understand that they will no longer be two individuals, but rather one unit expressing love toward God together. Marriage is more than a wedding; it is the expression of the sacrificial love of God. The wedding ceremony has a single purpose in which people commit to bring greater glory to God.

His Glory

God honors matrimony. He intends for our marriages to follow His model and bring forth glory to His name. Marriage is not just about finding someone that makes us smile or laugh. It is definitely not the solution that prohibits us from living alone. A marriage partner is not intended to be our roommate so we can have someone to help pay bills. Thus, we must be careful about the connections we make for marriage.

Consider the accomplishments we are able to make while we are single. Think about how much is learned when we are ourselves. Think about the opportunities we have to establish a stronger relationship with God without any interference. We should be mindful of the freedoms we have as single individuals and we should never take those opportunities for granted. In the same instance, we need to constantly evaluate our progression in ministry. As we evaluate all aspects of our life, we must consider whether our personal responses are reflective of glory being given to God in our lives; for we are designed to give Him glory.

Our individual life is not for self-serving purposes. The blessings we receive in our life are for the benefit of giving glory to God. Although we make plans and create daily agendas, our life is not premised upon the fulfillment of our personal will. We were created to bless the name of the Lord. His agenda is completed with one item specification: God be glorified. In the midst of receiving glory from us, God takes time to grant us things we want, but the marriage union does not change God's appetite for glory. Together, a husband and wife should give God more glory than would be offered as individuals.

God remains jealous. Therefore, men and women should never crave each other more than God. We should hunger and thirst after His righteousness (Matthew 5:6) and our appetite should remain unquenched any time God is not uplifted. Our fulfillment and joy comes from magnifying Him. Getting married does not give you joy, it takes your current state of joy to another level. First, we must know how to adhere to Christ. Once connected, we should desire to praise Him forever and our union will be eternal.

93

" *A*lot of discipline is required between now and the attainment of God's predestinated promise. We must train ourselves to control our urges. Waiting is not simple. Waiting entails self-regulatory measures. It is a training process that incorporates many steps of self-denial."

CHAPTER 6

. . . . . .

SINGLE URGES

Our personal desires for satisfaction affect our ability to patiently wait. We seek gratification without recognizing that quick fixes lead to greater delays. Society itself has become an incubator for instantaneous fulfillment. There is an abundance of messages that glamorize our indulgences and motivate us to partake in them immediately. The most simple of these may be to purchase a burger or high calorie ice cream, whereas others may solicit us to pay for expensive jewelry or real estate. But, do not leave out those enticing commercials that elude to companionship if we just buy the perfect perfume or lingerie. Each image is an attempt by an individual company to connect with our urges or desires.

For the sake of earning capital, companies purposely target our innermost desires. Our compulsive desire to eat fatty food, to own our own homes, to wear the finest things, or to be connected to someone who loves us are examples of desires that are easily marketed by companies. Each of us is susceptible to being lured in directions that allow us to attain immediate gratification. After all, who wants to wait for something they can have immediately? The same is true about those things we want from relationships. We enter into dangerous, unfulfilling companionship because we prefer to have someone now instead of waiting for the potential greatness that could be coming in our future.

No one likes uncertainty. We want houses, cars, jewelry, jobs, children and mates to be predictable facets of our life story. For many of us, waiting is symbolic of uncertainty and possibly unfulfilled dreams. In some cases, people hold on to hope, but become weary because the wait seems so long. While in line for their blessing, they see others who find contentment and it serves as a reminder of their waiting process. Unfortunately, many people become impatient, jealous and sometimes troubled by what seems to be an unfair delay to true happiness.

A lot of discipline is required between now and the attainment of God's predestinated promise. We must train ourselves to control our urges. Waiting is not simple. Waiting entails self-regulatory measures. It is a training process that incorporates many steps of self-denial. A person in waiting cannot focus on cravings for connection with a husband or wife. He or she cannot overindulge in the need for attention or constantly be thirsty for pleasure. These urges will cause a person to surrender the best of themselves at the most inappropriate time. Regret is usually the end result.

The most tantalizing urge is to be loved. However, the wish to be loved should not be substituted with the desire to be touched. A physical touch does not necessarily suggest love. Sometimes, we prematurely enter into relationships with others who hold our hands, stroke our hair, or gently kiss our lips. None of these actions mean we are loved by them. They can be as empty as spoken words. Even titles like boyfriend, girlfriend, fiancé, and in some cases, husband or wife can be void of true affection. Love is not about the touch. It is not about urges of men and women being satisfied. If that were the case, people who had the best pick-up lines, crafty words, or sensual sexual affairs would exhibit the most gratifying and successful relationships.

Generally, our physical urges lead to more trouble than satisfaction. Let us have an honest conversation about those things which are often overlooked in pulpits and singles' ministries. Before picking up this book, many already knew about the dangers of connecting with people before God's intended timing. Many realize problems can arise when we hurriedly enter relationships using our own timetable rather than waiting for the perfect timing created by God, however, we often remain unsure of what to do about the urges we have while we wait on His perfectly planned moment. How do we deal with the cravings we have for connection? What happens when our body is hankering for pleasure and lusts after physical enjoyment?

Whether virgins or not, our bodies can be the biggest weapon used to combat our patience. The lusts of our flesh seek to fulfill urges that we may not know how to control. Virgins are constantly wondering about the sexual nature glorified in television shows, movies, and personal conversations. The stories invoke interest and curiosity about sexual activity. Unmarried individuals who have participated in sexual activity are victims of memories and desire for perpetual stimulation. People who are well into childbearing years are further pressured by bodies that yearn to complete the actions necessary for pregnancy. Yet, neither gender should give themselves to their sexual cravings. We must learn how to turn off inflamed urges and remain in position for our blessing.

We have to say, "No!" to ourselves. Making that declaration is not an easy task. It requires major support. When the single urge to have sex arises, more than a cold shower is required. Single people have to stay in prayer and committed to reading the word of God. Singles need to be connected with other God-fearing people who they can honestly talk to when they are struggling with urges. When their bodies are working against them, singles need other activities like shopping, exercising, bowling, and other personal high interest hobbies. It may be most reasonable to delete the phone numbers of those they are most attracted to. Those with the strongest sex drives typically suffer longest with feelings of desired intimacy and must stay communed with God for help.

As single people, we should not put ourselves in compromising positions by trusting ourselves too much. Spending long periods of time alone with persons we are attracted to is unwise. We cannot make wagers that our love for God will keep us from making stupid mistakes. Our bodies are strong weapons. They are like guns and our yearnings are the bullets contained within. Placing ourselves in close-quarter situations for extended periods of time is like pulling the trigger on our sex drive. Many people who believed they could overcome such predicaments, thinking they could handle simple things like kissing, caressing, stroking, and touching eventually recognized the power of flesh.

Only those who want to be kept by God can be kept. God will not force His will on those who do not want to accept His grace. Some singles want to do their own thing; thereby, choosing to fulfill their lustful desires, but later having to deal with the feelings of dissatisfaction, unhappiness, isolation, sorrow, and regret. Telling our body "No!" and preventing it from having what it desires may hurt. It will also leave us feeling further disconnected from love. However, at those moments we must keep in mind that physical attachment and love are not synonymous.

More than receiving love from others, we must have the urge to know ourselves. William Shakespeare said it best, "to thine own self be true," inspiring us to grow. Single people should realize the satisfaction that comes by first knowing how to love oneself and appreciating the person in the mirror. Unless we value ourselves as God does, we cannot expect others to see the worth God sees in us. We should treat ourselves to the things we deserve. Single people should not deny themselves the right to having a good time. It is okay to go to the movies alone or dine in a restaurant without being escorted. Our concerns cannot be conditioned upon what others think, but rather on our ability to enjoy personal company without limitations. We can go to a museum or attend a concert or a play, and have full enjoyment of the performance when we accept that we are worthy to enjoy life without a companion and know that our happiness is not predicated upon other individuals. In those moments, we learn to enjoy our own company and assess our likes and dislikes. At those times, we can appreciate life without the influence of the outside world. Imagine the honesty we are capable of yielding when the time comes for us to disengage from solidarity. Imagine, the expert knowledge we will have acquired about ourselves and the ease of our response when asked what we really like or dislike. The answer will not take a lot of guesswork; it will be an honest reflection of the moments we have been afforded to explore our full being during our time of singlehood.

"*Our single status is important to God. He molds us for successful partnership. He prepares us for blessed companionship if we use our time wisely. God is perfecting the smell and look of our bait. He is making us the authentic lure that will be reeled in by the right mate for life.*"

CHAPTER 7

......

THE HUNTER

The hunter pursues with the intent of doing so. Hunting is not a haphazard occurrence wherein a hunter stumbles upon its prey. A true hunter is looking for the object of his highest affection. In the case of marriage, the hunter is a man who desires and seeks after his wife. Unlike the sport, spiritual hunters are not looking to kill what is captured. Wives are not apprehended for the purpose of being eaten, but rather to be adored.

Best Season for the Hunter

In the state of Florida, duck hunters do not go outside and start looking for ducks in the month of May. Optimal hunting occurs between November and the end of January. Undoubtedly, it is better to hunt other animals in different seasons. But those looking for a duck, should hunt in duck season. My neighbor, who is an expert marksman in archery, hunts deer and competes nationally. Through conversation with him, I have learned that the Florida Fish and Wildlife Conservation Commission specifies when and where you are allowed to hunt as well as the type of weapons that may be used to capture prey. In fact, penalties are applied to those who take home something that is not permitted. The commission fines hunters who seek to capture wildlife out of season and also if the hunter is found in areas not permitted by hunting regulations.

Pending the species being hunted, opening season changes for the hunter. Of course, women are not pieces of meat to be hunted down like prey. Neither is the spiritual hunt for a good woman to be considered a game or sport. A man of God never has the intent of killing what he has hunted so that it may be devoured. He is considered more of a tracker who searches for the perfect treasure. He knows the best season to skillfully seek his wife; it is the season in which God has confirmed that he is complete, confident, and ready to lead. Through his relationship with Christ, a Godly man gears up and goes to permissible hunting territory on a quest for the right woman. His goal is to take home a wife, nothing more and nothing less. Looking for a mate in the wrong season may result in taking home the wrong species. Figuratively speaking, men hunting for ducks may go home with spring turkeys when their steps are not ordered by God (Psalms 37:23).

Best Bait

Sometimes fishermen are not categorized as hunters, but the concept of both sports is similar. Both sports require preparation. Identically, fisherman and hunters must be familiar with regulations and the demand for sporting licenses. Scouting the land to know what prey to expect in a particular territory is important. No one wants to waste their time trying to reach their goal in places where nothing thrives.

I love seafood, but do not care for the sport of fishing. I do not enjoy spending time trying to hook a sea creature on a pole just to scale, gut, clean and cook it later. I appreciate the end result, but do not enjoy the process.

I have plenty of family members and co-workers who enjoy fishing as a pastime. They typically talk about their enjoyment of either freshwater or saltwater fishing and whether they like fly fishing, piers, or using sail boats. Their conversations include the types of boats and kinds of bait used, but their greatest joy is always exemplified when they describe their biggest catch and the process used to reel in their prized fish. Fishermen never forget the bait they used to catch her! They have better chances catching "the big one" when they learn which bait is best. Not all fish will be lured by the bait.

If fishing is a foreign practice to you then you might not be aware that there are two types of bait, natural and artificial. Although single women are longing to be caught by the perfect man, we definitely should be weary of men fishing for wives using artificial bait. Sometimes our appetite for marriage will trick us into falling "hook, line, and sinker" for manufactured appeal. Fishermen use phony bait because it can be used repetitively. Remember, our single season is about getting in tune with the voice of God. Women should feel compelled to seek God about the authenticity of the bait used to reel us in. Hearing God prevents us from being one of many fish that were caught by the use of trickery and deception. The Bible forewarns us of being enticed by the snares of the enemy (Psalms 91:3 & Psalms 141:9). Just because the bait looks good does not mean it is good.

Artificial bait is 100 percent fake, but it looks good to most fish. It appears as a succulent snack that dangles in the water to serve as a reward for an unsuspecting hungry fish. Only particular fish are susceptible to artificial bait. Some fish will bypass the counterfeit because they can recognize the difference between real and pretend bait. Yet, some fishermen are a little more leery of using natural bait because it is costly. It can be frustrating for them to put their bait out and have it eaten by fish that are not successfully reeled in. Their dissatisfaction is like that of the man who shares his authentic self with the woman he hopes to pledge his undying love upon, when no schemes are used, but rejection becomes his reality.

Natural relationships are unpretentious. Like men hunting for the ideal wife, fishermen know what they are fishing for when they set sail or stand at the shore. Men are as vulnerable as women. They also pray that the spiritual nature they have protected during their time of singleness will not be overlooked. When men finally decide to cast the rod of their true fragile character, they want their sacrifice to be honored. Surely, every fish will not be attracted, but ideally the special one will draw near until she is hooked and reeled in.

Good bait will entice fish to bite even when the fisherman has no desire to catch it. We know it is easy to throw back something we dislike and have no desire for, but what if we are inclined to believe it will bring us great satisfaction? For instance, a fisherman hooks a 20 pound bass that he has always dreamed of catching. After reeling in the huge fish, he is told to return it to the water or he will be heavily fined. While the fisherman may hesitate before giving up the awesome catch; the fine makes the dream risky to keep. Like fishermen, Godly men must be patient and willing to wait on the right catch in the right season. Men must wait on the woman who brings spiritual benefits, not costs. Thus, he must be willing to throw some back into the sea.

God knows if certain women are reeled in during a particular season of a man's life, the outcome will not benefit either party. Without question, some women do not belong in a man's life during a certain period of time (if at all) and the reciprocal is true. As important as timing is in fishing and hunting, exactness of the hour is equally paramount when connecting two individuals.

Our single status is important to God. He molds us for successful partnership. He prepares us for blessed companionship if we use our time wisely. God is perfecting the smell and look of our bait. He is making us the authentic lure that will be reeled in by the right mate for life. If our time alone is spent honoring God, He will use that time teaching us how to avoid fines and penalties that break our heart. We cannot get ahead of ourselves and see dating as a game that we can perfect by ourselves. Without Christ, we set ourselves up for heartbreak and disaster.

It has taken my neighbor years to perfect his craft, with the bow and arrow, but now he can shoot an arrow from his bow and hit the target dead center from 50 feet away. As we allow God to perfect us during our singleness, we will approach the juncture where the union we seek will be perfect.

*L*ife Quotes

• • •

"Being single isn't a time to be looking for love,
use that time to work on yourself
and grow as an individual."

"*The wounds of our past have the potential to restrain us. Our former discomfort may enslave us if we allow it to overcome us. Many single people are unsure how to unfasten themselves from the grip of emotional bruises. Thus, they enter new relationships while in an emotional drought.*"

CHAPTER 8

• • • • • •

ENSLAVED

The consideration of marriage requires us to search for the honest response to the question, "What are we prepared to contribute to a lifelong relationship?" Marriage is more than a feel good occurrence that leaves us with pretty wedding pictures to be framed and perfectly hung over a mantle. It is a sacred merging of two lives to create a sustainable partnership for the glory of God. Marriage depends upon sacrifice, negating our usual tendency to hope selfish desires will be fulfilled. Marriage is not the answer to getting what we want from someone else every day. A prerequisite for marriage is to ensure we are not in an emotional drought, enslaved to negative feelings from past relationships and unequipped to enrich the present relationship. Each person should be capable of pouring goodness into the union God has called together (two people married to experience an elevated sense of purpose and shift toward the harvest of spiritual fruit and prosperity).

While single, some persons experience the shackles of damaging "love" relationships. Unfortunately, the love of God is missing as the foundation. As a result, some become disenfranchised by poor communication, deprived of spiritual support, physically and emotionally abused, and confined to loneliness while supposedly connected to another individual. The emotional wounds we suffer often reduce us to places of spiritual bondage. We become incapable of giving fully and have limited capacity to operate in our next relationship with clarity. Negative emotions mentally incarcerate us, keeping us enslaved to the hope of getting what we want the next time around. Unsurprisingly, those selfish desires are the very things that prohibit us from reaching our goal. Before we can say "I do," we have to become liberated from past hurts.

The pain suffered while single does not always come from a previous boyfriend or girlfriend. The relationships that injure us can be from family ties and the brokenness created by our mothers and fathers. Issues that develop with our closest friends can be crippling agents that prevent us from moving forward freely. Emotional baggage can keep us from revealing our whole self to our life-long spouse. Instead of sharing the God-ordained, 100 percent version of our unique greatness, we give them a tarnished incomplete adaptation, while our greater self hides beneath the layers of affliction, subdued by the encounters of yesterday.

The wounds of our past have the potential to restrain us. Our former discomfort may enslave us if we allow it to overcome us. Many single people are unsure how to unfasten themselves from the grip of emotional bruises. Thus, they enter new relationships while in an emotional drought. They have nothing to contribute to a strong foundation. They have nothing to give toward the positive expansion of love. An emotional drought is a state of barrenness. Those experiencing such a dry spell have an extremely low ability to engage in the exchange of positive feelings for an extended period of time. They constantly hope for a rainfall of happiness and look for someone else to replenish them.

Relationships do not work when one person constantly seeks attention and is always in need of receiving deposits of affection. We must build our emotional bank accounts before marriage, having enough stability to make sentimental withdrawals that will not injure ourselves or our partner. Many single people have overdrawn emotional accounts. Scars from previous relationships make them inefficient with handling love and leave people with major deficits in regards to the way they care for themselves, let alone how to care for a spouse. During our season of singlehood, God provides us with time to repair our emotional accounts. Our Heavenly Father is capable of teaching us how to overcome the drought.

When we avail ourselves to the plan of God, He helps us gain awareness about ourselves and our needs. God comes to mend the brokenhearted (Psalms 147:3, Luke 4:18, & Isaiah 61:1). He prepares us to encourage and uplift others. He establishes us and makes us ready to be a blessing not a burden. Rather than having grudges about our current state of singleness, we should evaluate our emotional bank accounts and reflect upon our level of readiness to give a future mate an eternal partnership. Only our relationship with Christ can truly prepare us for this type of investment. Jesus is the only one who can set a standard for a relationship characterized by freedom, sacrifice, and unconditional love. There is no form of bondage in our union with Him.

Many people believe their previous relationships prepare them for marriage. Unfortunately, in some cases those relationships actually hinder their future. Past involvements may create damaging situations or yield pain that is hard to escape. We become enslaved by thoughts about what has occurred.

We fearfully brace ourselves for future pain as we are conditioned by our experience. Exposure to hurt has the capacity to control and dominate our thinking and expectations. This phenomenon explains why women who are accustomed to abuse expect mistreatment by everyone she encounters. It further explains why boys who have been molested, build emotional walls to guard themselves from a world of mistrust that they believe lurk in our society. Imagine how this type of pain can lead to problems in a relationship if left unrevealed and unaddressed.

We cannot expect that intimate relationships with people will fix our former trauma. Spouses are not emotional surgeons certified to mend our wounds. It is our responsibility as single men and women to bring our fragile concerns to Christ. It is imperative for us to surrender to the Lord and ask for His help to resolve emotional issues before we marry someone. Otherwise, it is likely that our spouse will be married to an enslaved soul for a good portion of the union. Couples exchange nuptials thinking they will enter years of marital bliss, only to find that their partner is a bondservant to unrevealed agony. One or the other, and sometimes both parties, could feasibly be the product of emotional turmoil and misguided thinking. In which case, they may be enslaved, controlled by feelings and emotions not yet resolved.

It is amazing how many people believe they will be freed from their life of internal misery when they get married. They trust in the idea of being rescued by our man-made definition of love. Some earnestly equate their wedding day as the debut event for personal freedom. The caged heart is perceived to be released by the sound of wedding bells. Unfortunately, weddings are not the keys to emotional jails.

Hoping for a spouse to free us is really transitioning negative authority over to another person. Whenever we yield our authority to someone else, we give them power over us. Thus, we should not believe a spouse has the power to release us from our burdens. We should empower ourselves, through faith in Christ, to declare our personal freedom. We must be accountable to ourselves, and embrace spiritual power to live freely. Singleness is a time to acquire emotional independence, making ourselves ready to be matched with another unchained soul.

Life Quotes

● ● ●

"Don't be reckless with other people's hearts, don't put up with people who are reckless with yours."

" *Preparation is required for the melding of two souls. Each individual endures training in the field of sacrifice before being joined together. When each soul has accepted the benefits of living in total union with God, the individual becomes better prepared to connect with a soulmate.*"

CHAPTER 9

......

SOUL TRAINING

Your single life is the ultimate training ground for marriage when you are solely connected to the greatest love of all time– Jesus. Your communion with Him prepares you for a future with your husband or wife and keeps that relationship from going astray.

Many marriages dissolve because the focus is on tangible items or because spouses do not know how to repair hurt feelings. Those marriages are in bad shape because, in many cases, the partners were only tied together by what they believed they could attain together or by an emotional bond. Marriages lack strength when the soul connection that links couples spiritually is limited or altogether missing. Marriages can be further damaged when each spouse does not possess the skills to overcome mundane issues. Long lasting relationships are connected from the soul, whereby Jesus rests at the center, and serves as the chief cornerstone of the union.

Marital connections should not be reliant upon the fact that mates think alike. Similarities should not be the primary purpose for connecting with someone else. We must be careful about biblical principles that forewarn us about how like spirits attract themselves to one another. Thus, foolishness will attract itself to foolishness in the same manner as poverty, depression, aggression, and lying spirits attract themselves. None of these attributes need a connecting partner that will help foster growth because they are all negative. Similarly, great sexual connections are not a sign of the perfect union. No merit can be given to sexual unions that appear to bring great pleasure since body types and sex drives change over time. More spiritual substance is needed to establish a lasting relationship. There must be a soul connection. We should be able to genuinely sing the lyrics to the gospel song that says, "The Jesus in You, Loves the Jesus in Me."

Preparation is required for the melding of two souls. Each individual endures training in the field of sacrifice before being joined together. When each soul has accepted the benefits of living in total union with God, the individual becomes better prepared to connect with a soulmate. It pleases God to join men and women who have loved Him first. He wants us to cleave to one another, forsaking mother and father; leave the natural support and nourishment of this world and create a soul connection of united purpose (Genesis 2:24). The spiritual purpose of man and woman is linked so the plan of God may be fulfilled.

So many single people are overwhelmed by the desire to be married. Their goal to have a mate blinds them to the overall intention of marriage. If our dreams of marriage only include houses, white picket fences, children and pets, then I am afraid we have missed the spiritual mark and should not be surprised at the number of marriages that fail. Although Christ wants us to be happy and to be blessed with our desires, His death was not intended for us to obtain selfish desire, notoriety or be married by a certain date on the calendar. His sacrifice was not endured so we can attain a desired status or experience emotional bliss. The death, burial, and resurrection of Christ destroyed iniquity and opened the door to abundance.

Do not be captivated by the joyful sights of wedding gowns, diamond rings, photographs, and receptions. Our wedding day should not be the primary emphasis in our life. Getting married is not the cornerstone of success, nor is it the tipping point for life achievement. The act of getting married does not mean we finally have hit the jackpot of plenty and will live lavishly. The abundance that Christ died for us to receive can be attained while we are single. Living life abundantly is to live with the fruit of the spirit abounding. To have abundance is to have true love, joy, peace, longsuffering, gentleness, goodness, faith, meekness and temperance overflowing in life (Galatians 5:22-23).

When each mate merges with another person who possesses those spiritual characteristics, then they are capable of living life bountifully in the union of marriage. Unfortunately, because so many people fail to focus on those qualities and replace them with less Godly attributes, their marriages are declared dysfunctional. Because they enter marriage with spiritual deficits, they must learn to overcome their combined shortcomings. Added pressure is placed on marriages that begin with fragmented individuals. To this end, our single season allows us to become whole and filled with Godly character, which carries great value.

Two fragmented individuals might presume they can become complete when they are joined together. They may believe that the better half of each person will contribute to the perfection of their marriage. However, we should consider that the weaknesses of each half could just as easily contribute to the failure of the union; thereby, creating a complete mockery of all they try to accomplish. As singles, we must evaluate whether our goal is to seek the possibility of effectiveness or the promise of excellence.

I pray our answer is excellence. Wait on it! Christ has not forgotten you. If you allow Him, He will perfect you and bring you into a more perfect union. Appreciate this time you have to get to know yourself and your Savior. Appreciate this season that God is taking to fashion you as a better mate whose union will be longstanding. Entering this level of ministry without preparation will require you to fight demons that you were never trained to battle. On the contrary, allowing God to get everything set for your imminent abundance will more than satisfy you, and bring Him the glory.

Marriage is not as much about us as we think. Wait! Heed instruction! Train for the best! What God has in store for you is worth the time. You are worth the wait. Remember, there is purpose for you being single, and there is a single purpose for your life–That His glory may abound.

BIBLIOGRAPHY

Florida Fish and Wildlife Conservation Commission (1999-2016). Retrieved December 14, 2014 from myfwc.com

Franklin, K. (2006, March 25). "Love" Lyrics. Let's Sing It. Retrieved December 7, 2014 from http://artists.letssingit.com/kirkfranklin-lyrics-love-b4fhhbm#xzz2pM9hJbCL

Robinson, Cynthia. Mistress of Ceremony Comments from 12th Annual Jurisdictional Women's Convention. First Baptist Church of Apopka. 24-26 Sept. 2014.

About The Author

Dr. Anntwanique Edwards is a native of Connecticut. She is the eldest of three girls born to Jeffrey and Beverly Edwards. After graduating high school, she relocated to Gainesville, Florida and began studies at the University of Florida (UF).

Dr. Edwards earned each of her degrees from UF, including a bachelor's degree in sociology and master's in counselor education. Additionally, she earned an educational specialist degree in counselor education with an emphasis on mental health counseling and second master's degree in educational leadership. In 2012, she attained a doctorate in educational leadership with a concentration in elementary and secondary administration. Dr. Edwards has worked as a mental health counselor, as well as a middle and high school guidance counselor, before serving in her current role as an assistant principal in the public school system. She is licensed by the Church of God in Christ (COGIC) as a missionary evangelist.

Dr. Edwards is a member of Unity Tabernacle, COGIC in Ocala, FL. She is a faithful member of her church and jurisdiction. She has a passion for working with youth and serves as the Youth Department Chairlady for Florida Central Second Ecclesiastical Jurisdiction. Additionally, Dr. Edwards is the coordinator for Sister2Sister, a commission under the COGIC International Youth Department (IYD). She is the founder and former pastor of Generation COGIC. Furthermore, she is the founder and president of Divine Ministry, Inc. (www.divineministry.net), a non-profit organization that offers academic scholarships, financial literacy workshops, and resources to disadvantaged women and children.

Dr. Edwards is the author of "Daddy, Where are You?" as well as "Where is Thy Faith?" Her writing and evangelistic heart have afforded her the opportunity to minister in Gaborone, Botswana, Africa; Montego Bay and Kingston, Jamaica; and Montrouis, Haiti. Also, she joined in co-authoring a Sister2Sister IYD publication, Symphony of Sisterhood. Although she has been favored to receive many positions, her desire is to be recognized as a true woman of God who loves Him with her whole heart.

CONTACT THE AUTHOR

Please email or write the author with any comments you may have. You are also welcome to contact her for bookings. Dr. Edwards is available for book club presentations, book signings, or speaking engagements for your church or organization (women's ministries, women's clubs, conferences, workshops, retreats, and seminars).

Contact her at:

Anntwanique Edwards
divineministry05@gmail.com
Phone: (888) 907-2237
P.O. Box 358527
Gainesville, FL 32635-8527